Ice Cream Shop Tycoon

Flexible, No-Prep, Standards-based PBL Project

PBL Central

Project-Based Learning Simplified

Ice Cream Shop Tycoon Project

Welcome to the Ice Cream Shop Tycoon PBL project.

In this project, your learners design an ice cream shop that will be ready to compete with the best ice cream shops operating in your local city. Students will consider all aspects of business start-up including menu design and branding, customer experience, pricing and costs, marketing, etc.

There is a wealth of information in this packet to guide you and your students through an amazing learning experience. Whether you are an experienced PBL teacher or trying PBL for the first time, this resource contains everything you need to feel confident in supporting your learners throughout the project.

The main components of this resource are:

Teacher Guide

Provides all the information required to get you started on the Ice Cream Shop Tycoon PBL project.

Learning Content Modules

Provides the content you need to guide your students through the various stages of business design.

Learning Standards

Contains the extensive list of learning standards that this project encompasses. Specific standards for language arts, social studies, career preparation, technology and design, math and art are included.

All you need to do now is get started and enjoy the journey with your students!

What is PBL & Why Use It?

If you're new to PBL, this section is for you.

Project-based learning is not 'doing projects.'

A **project** is a task that students complete after learning content in order to demonstrate understanding.

In **project-based learning**, students are given a real-world problem that engages and motivates them. Through the process of exploring and engaging with the issue, students discover the need to learn specific content and skills because that knowledge is required to solve the problem.

Students become more engaged with learning because the motivation is driven from their need to know. Your role becomes more of a coach to guide your students to the best learning resources to meet their needs. (In many cases the best learning resources might be you - but now students are asking you for the information, instead of you telling your students what they need to know.)

Because of the student-centred drive for information, PBL projects not only build independent learning skills, but also develop essential critical thinking, communication and collaboration skills.

PBL projects have the potential to be the most memorable and most effective of your students' school experiences. Get started now!

Ice Cream Shop Tycoon

Table of Contents

1. Teacher Guide

Introduction

This Teacher Guide contains everything you need to plan your ice cream shop project in a quick 30 minutes.

You will select your driving question, identify your launch and culminating events, and decide which of the five available modules you will include in the project.

Following the teacher introduction, you will find the individual learning content modules, each with extensive teacher- and student-directed resources.

Project Planning Checklist

Preparing for your project is easy. Simply review the list below, read the relevant sections in this Teacher Guide, and complete the worksheet on the next page. Once you have done that, you are ready to go!

- ☐ Edit the driving question to suit the needs of your students and to identify the specific city/town for the ice cream shops.

- ☐ Decide what your launch event will be.

- ☐ Plan the format and audience for the culminating event.

- ☐ Decide which modules you will include in the project.

- ☐ Plan major milestones.

- ☐ Identify student resources.

- ☐ Plan for assessment and check-in.

- ☐ Consider the needs of first-time PBL classes.

Complete the worksheet below and keep it handy for your reference.

Project Planning Worksheet

Project Name:

Driving Question:

Launch Event:

Culminating Event:

Modules to Include + Schedule (approx. # of classes or completion date)

- ☐ Launch Event
- ☐ Naming, Branding & Menu ___________
- ☐ Workspace Layout ___________
- ☐ Customer Experience ___________
- ☐ Pricing & Costing ___________
- ☐ Marketing ___________
- ☐ Culminating Event ___________

____

Resource Sources:

Assessment:

Note: Full-size versions of all worksheets are located at the end of the document for easy printing.

Planning Step 1: Identify Your Driving Question

In a PBL, the Driving Question introduces a simply stated real world issue or dilemma. The driving question must be inherently engaging for your students in order to drive their motivation to discuss, inquire and investigate the topic.

Below you will find a range of driving questions appropriate for this project. Each lends itself to a different grade-level range, depth of study and possible end products. Replace italicized phrases with a location relevant to your community.

1. A mysterious investor wants to invest in an ice cream shop business in *your local city*. How can you convince the investor that you have the best idea for a successful ice cream shop?

2. How can I design a successful ice cream shop for *my local city*?

3. How can I design an ice cream shop that will be famous for its uniqueness?

4. How can I design an ice cream shop that produces little waste?

5. How can I design an ice cream shop for people on lactose-free, gluten-free, or vegan diets?

Once you have determined an appropriate driving question, note it on your planning worksheet.

Planning Step 2: Plan Your Launch Event

The launch event is your opportunity to get your students excited about the project. Make sure the event is fun and engaging. Be sure to avoid dumping a bunch of project requirements and instructions on your students. That is a sure-fire way to kill engagement.

See below for some options to spark your thinking.

Video	The videos listed below offer a variety of perspectives on ice cream shops. Choose one that suits the age/interests of your students.
Field Trip	A field trip to try out different ice cream shops is an excellent way to ignite your students' interest and motivation.
Guest Speaker	Consider inviting an ice cream shop owner to talk to your class.

Note your launch event decision on the project planning worksheet.

You can find more guidance on holding your launch event in the Launch Event module.

Video List

Please review videos in their entirety to ensure they are suitable for your students.

Taste Tour: 3 Super-Cool Ice Cream Shops Around the U.S (3 min)
https://geni.us/icecreamvideo1

The Best Ice Cream Parlors in Los Angeles (15 min)
https://geni.us/icecreamvideo2

3 Ice Cream Recipes COMPARED (5 mins vs 4 hours vs 7 hours)
https://geni.us/icecreamvideo3

How to start an ice cream business (frozen dessert business) (3 min)
https://geni.us/icecreamvideo4

Robyn Sue Fisher: Chief Ice Cream Maker (5 min)
https://geni.us/icecreamvideo5

How to start an ice cream business (6 min)
https://geni.us/icecreamvideo6

How to Start an Ice Cream Business Part 1 (12 min)
https://geni.us/icecreamvideo7

Planning Step 3: Determine Audience and Format for Culminating Event

The purpose of the culminating event is to showcase your students' work to an audience, whether that be student peers, other classes or staff, parents or community members.

Below you will find some suggestions for a culminating event. The best choice will depend on the driving question you chose.

Ice Cream Shop Fair

> Hold an ice cream shop fair in your classroom. Let your students display their ice cream shop materials for an audience of classmates, peers, or parents. The audience can be given a budget to spend at the ice cream shops.

Ice Cream Shop Field Trip

> If you haven't already found a reason to visit some ice cream shops during the project, the culminating day is an excellent opportunity.

Business Plan Presentation

> For those classes that have produced something closer to a real business plan, an excellent culminating event is to invite an ice cream shop entrepreneur or small-business investor or loans manager to class to listen to the students' business presentations.

For help planning your culminating event, see the Culminating Event module. For now, note your preferred ideas on your planning worksheet.

Planning Step 4: Choose Modules to Include

This project provides a large amount of flexibility. Include just a few modules for a quicker project with younger students. Include all modules for a longer, more in-depth project with older students.

Available Modules

Launch Event:

>This module steps you through an effective and fun project launch.

Name, Menu & Branding

>What is the name of my business and what will I serve?

Workspace Layout

>How can I design my shop layout so I can store food safely and prepare orders quickly?

Customer Experience: shop design, menu design, supporting items, music, etc.

>What will the complete buying experience be for my customers? (What will they see, hear, smell, do as they approach the shop and come inside and make a purchase?)

Pricing and Costing

>What will my ingredients cost and how should I price my menu?

Marketing

>How will my customers hear and find out about my business?

Culminating Event

>Steps you through an awesome project finale.

Once you have decided on the preferred modules, add the information to your planning worksheet.

Planning Step 5: Plan Major Milestones

The amount of time you have available will dictate the level of depth of your students' learning. More time will allow your learners to develop stronger inquiry and independent learning skills.

Think about how much time you can dedicate to each module and note down a rough estimate on your planning worksheet.

Within each of the content modules you will find resources for leading students into a deeper learning experience.

Planning Step 6: Identify Student Resources

During an inquiry-led PBL project, students will constantly be coming up with questions and need-to-knows. Some of these will be addressed by mini-lessons or other direct instruction. However, whenever possible, encourage your learners to seek the answers and the knowledge themselves.

To make this possible, you will need to supply sufficient resources so that your learners can gain skills in seeking and finding knowledge.

Ideally, your students will have access to the web to conduct research. If internet access is not a possibility, supply sufficient grade-appropriate, alternative resources such as books and videos about ice cream shops and relevant related topics such as start-up businesses, branding, marketing, etc.

Think about how your students will access the information they need for this project. Note your plans on your project worksheet.

          Ice Cream Shop Tycoon 

Planning Step 7: Determine Check-in & Assessment Methods

It is extremely important to include many check-in points during a project. This helps students stay aligned to the purpose of the project and allows you to identify any shortcomings that might need direct instruction via a mini-lesson.

For this reason, we suggest you include several of the following in each module to gauge and/or assess progress towards meeting the learning standards:

Regular and scheduled meetings with each group.

Typical questions you can ask during regular and ad-hoc meetings are:

- What are you working on?

- What is your goal?

- How will you know when you are done?

- How long do you think it will take you?

- What problems have you solved already?

- What problems do you still have?

- What are your ideas for solving that problem?

- What information would make it easy to solve this problem?

Module-specific check-in questions can also be found in each content module.

Interim assessments

Use interim assessments such as quizzes, homework assignments and quick-writes, to test content knowledge.

Keep in mind, assessments that do not contribute directly to the end
product will diminish the 'like real life' aspect of the overall project and
may affect engagement.

Reflection Points

Make sure to allow time for reflection at the end of each
module. Reflections are an important part of the PBL process as they
allow students to deepen their learning via a thoughtful review of the
content, methods and/or motivations for their learning

Each module contains reflection questions for your use.

Class-developed Progress Assessment Tools

Just as a PBL project shifts the ownership of learning from the teacher to
the student, we support a similar shifting of ownership of assessment from
teacher to the student.

As explained in Cooper & Murphy (2016)[1], students who shape how they
are assessed take ownership of their learning, which is the primary goal of
the PBL approach.

We encourage you to include class time in each module for facilitating
the development of an assessment guide, with the goal of developing
criteria for what an 'excellent project' looks like.

Once students own and understand the benchmark they are aiming for,
you will be impressed at their dedication to meeting the criteria.

Below you will find a sample rubric. Note the use of the first person so students
can identify with it more easily.

Reflect on your assessment needs and note your plans on the worksheet.

---

[1] Cooper, R. & Murphy, E. (2016) *Hacking Project Based Learning*. Times 10 Publications, Ohio.

     Ice Cream Shop Tycoon 

Research & Information Gathering	☐ My research included a variety of sources. ☐ I kept a list of the resources I used. ☐ I referenced my resources so that I know where information came from. ☐ My notes are organized and easy to use.
End Product	☐ The end product I created answered the driving question. ☐ My project conveyed information clearly and in a well-organized way. ☐ My project was free of errors.
Presentation Skills	☐ I conveyed all the important information when I presented my project. ☐ I acted confident when I presented my project. ☐ I looked at the audience when I presented my project. ☐ I answered questions about my project.
Revisions & Iterations	☐ I sought feedback on my project and listened. ☐ I considered feedback and edited my project to take it into account. ☐ I self-edited my project to find ways to improve it.
Collaboration & Teamwork	☐ I listened and contributed during group discussions. ☐ I helped resolve differing opinions. ☐ I completed the tasks I was assigned by the group.

Planning Step 8: Consider First Time PBL Classes

If your students have not participated in a PBL project before, you may need to educate them about what to expect. Several key elements are:

1. You don't know everything you need to know to do the project. You will be learning it as you go along.

    One of the key skills you will develop by doing a PBL is knowing what information you need to learn.

2. You will iterate.

    As you learn more during a PBL, you will realize you need to reconsider some earlier decisions you made. You will probably iterate through several revisions as you proceed through the project. This is how real-world projects progress and needing to revise is a sign of progress, not failure.

3. Your group members will have different thoughts and opinions from you.

    Working through different opinions to reach a consensus is another valuable skill that PBLs help develop.

If you are new to PBL yourself, don't worry! The materials in this packet will provide everything you need to feel comfortable with diving into the project.

That's it for planning. Read on and learn more about the individual content modules.

Ice Cream Shop Tycoon 

2. Module Intro Guide

This project contains seven modules: the launch event module, the culminating event module and five learning content modules.

The launch event module steps you through the process of providing a fun and engaging entry event to ignite the interest of your students, introduces the driving question and gets your students started on their learning journey.

The culminating event module provides the resources you need for a meaningful and satisfying conclusion to the project.

The bulk of this project packet contains resources for the learning content modules. Each content module contains:

Module Topic

Specifies the topic for this module.

End Products

Specifies the end product that the students will produce.

Teacher & Student Resources

There are two types of resources in each module: Student-directed worksheets and reflections, and teacher-directed guidance.

Resources for you to distribute to your students include:

1. **Brainstorming worksheets** covering key elements in the topic.

   Use these worksheets to stimulate student thinking and help learners consider the relevant issues for each of the topics.

2. **Reflection worksheets**

   Reflections are an important part of the PBL process as they allow students to deepen their learning via a thoughtful review of the content, methods and/or motivations for their learning.

If your students are independent and motivated, you may not need to use any of the brainstorming resources. Instead let them dive into the PBL project, making sure to check in with them regularly to ensure they are on track.

If your students need more scaffolding, pick and choose from the worksheets to encourage the depth of learning that will most benefit your students.

The student-directed resources can be found at the end of each module.

The teacher-directed resources in each module include:

1   **Driving Questions**

   Although your students have been introduced to the project driving question during the launch event, some may need a little direction for how to get started with each module.

   Use the provided module-specific driving questions to provide a first level of scaffolding for students.

2   **Check-in Questions**

   Check-in questions are used during regular check-in/reporting sessions to ensure your learners are on track and not heading off in the wrong direction.

       Ice Cream Shop Tycoon 

Use the provided module-specific check-in questions as a guide during your scheduled and ad-hoc meetings.

3 'Deepen the Learning' Options

When students are new to PBL or not fully engaged with the topic, their learning can be shallow as they quickly try to reach the endpoint.

We've got you covered in dealing with this all-too-common problem. Each content module contains 3-5 easy options for helping your learners stretch their thinking and engage with the topic in more depth.

These include:

- **Discussion Points**

  Deepen the Learning discussion points are questions to help learners go beyond their initial thinking and consider aspects of the learning task that they may not have considered. Use these for your whole class or for individual groups who need help engaging with the topic.

- **Introduce/Encourage Professional Software**

  Encourage a grade-level appropriate method for creating the end products. If you have sufficient access to tablets or computers, consider encouraging your older students to use popular software tools such Canva for design, Wix Logo Maker for designing logos, etc.

  Familiarity with a variety of software tools builds your students' digital literacy and increases engagement.

- **Competition Analysis**

  Investigating how other ice cream shop owners have made similar decisions is a great way to help students think harder about their own decisions.

In most module you will find one or more worksheets that encourage your learners to critically evaluate their competitors.

- **First Draft Review and Reiteration**

  Require learners to present their draft ideas to the class or small group for review. Allow time for revision. This step has multiple benefits.

  - Students learn to critically evaluate other's work and provide meaningful feedback.

  - Students learn to present ideas-in-progress and graciously receive feedback. This is a different experience to presenting a final presentation.

Use one or more of these deepen the learning options to really engage your students and make this project their most memorable yet.

4 Scheduling Guide

Use the information in this section to gain an accurate understanding of the scheduling requirements for each module. The project is extremely flexible. Each module could take as little as one class period or extend with more in-depth learning for 1-2 weeks.

5 Mini-lesson Resources

Mini-lessons are 5-15 minutes of direct instruction covering information that you or your students have identified as necessary in order to move forward.

Each module contains a list of possible mini-lessons and associated resources.

3. Launch Event Module

This module steps you through the launch event that you planned during your initial project preparation.

Launch Event Checklist

Use the following checklist to guide the flow of your launch event.

☐ Present the fun video / introduce guest speaker

☐ Introduce your driving question/scenario

☐ Facilitate initial discussion & planning

    o Identify project components

    o Identify questions & need-to-knows

    o Introduce the culminating event

    o Identify available resources

☐ Divide students into groups

☐ Confirm students' initial goals and first check-in

Present Video/Guest Speaker

Get your students motivated by presenting the fun launch video, guest speaker
or field trip. For in-class experiences, consider how you can bring more
excitement to the event by:

- Adding music

- Providing popsicles or ice cream cones

- Displaying sample menus or photos from local ice cream shops

Introduce Your Driving Question

After showing the video/listening to the guest speaker, introduce the driving
question. Let your students discuss it, ask questions and wonder about it. Use this
discussion to segue into your initial brainstorming (see below).

NOTE: Your students will need to think about the driving question over a period
of days/weeks/months. Post the question in your classroom so it is highly visible
to your students both when they are working on the project and at other times.

Facilitate Initial Discussion & Brainstorming

After introducing the driving question, maintain your learner's enthusiasm by
introducing one or more of the following key questions. Brainstorm these topics
as a class, in groups or in some variant of self-pair-share format.

Worksheets can be found at the end of this module.

          Ice Cream Shop Tycoon 

Brainstorm: What will I do/make/decide while planning my ice cream shop?

Use this question to help students analyze the tasks required in the project.

It is vital for students to have an understanding of where they are going – and how they will get there.

At this point, there is no need to reach a final decision on the exact format of their end products - depending on your driving question, your students may create a project board, video or formal business plan. Instead, you want your students to start thinking about where they might end up and what issues they might address on the journey.

Feel free to introduce your plans for the culminating event at this point. This will help students understand their goal more.

Brainstorm: What do I need to know?

A key step in PBL projects is for learners to take ownership of learning by determining their own knowledge gaps.

Brainstorm: Questions I have

Another way to stimulate students' independent learning is to support them in identifying questions they have.

Introduce the Culminating Event

If you have not already discussed it, complete the brainstorming session by letting your students know a few details about the culminating event.

For a culminating event like the ice cream shop fair, the information will let your students know of the fun coming their way, which will increase motivation for the project.

For a culminating event like a presentation to an ice cream shop entrepreneur or investor, the information will let your students know that they will be performing in front of an external audience. This will increase their investment in the project and their sense that they are working on something 'real'.

Discuss Available Resources

Educate students about the resources that are available to help them in their journey. These might include books collected in the classroom, access to the library, or guidance on accessing information via the web.

Form Groups

You may wish to form groups before brainstorming, but this is also a good time. Use your knowledge of the students to form groups of an appropriate size and composition.

This project works well as an individual task as well as in groups of 2-5.

Identify Initial Goals and Check-in

Now that your learners have an understanding of the scope of the project, you can support them in identifying what their first steps are to work towards the first milestone.

Encourage a high level of enthusiasm as you end the session.

Student Worksheets

Full-size worksheets for printing can be found at the end of this document.

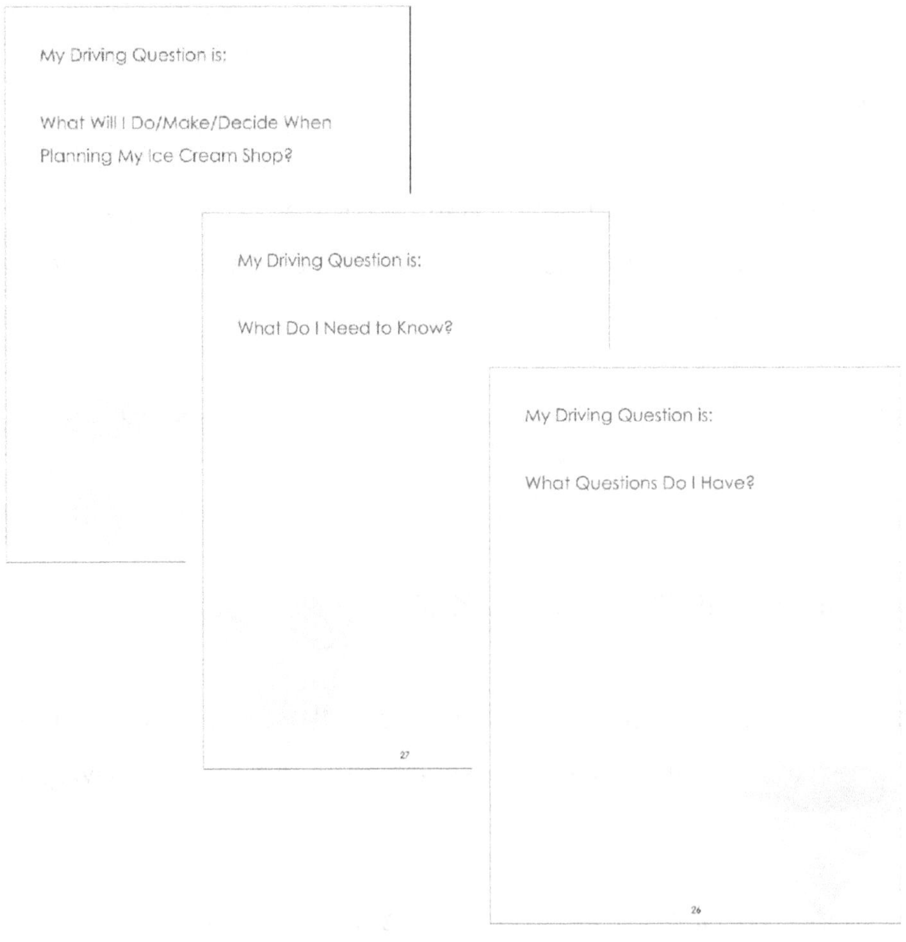

4. Name, Menu & Branding Module

Module Topic

This module contains resources for guiding your students through naming, branding and planning the menu items for their ice cream shop.

End Products

The products of this module are:

    * Ice cream shop name   * Menu items   * Logo & tagline

Teacher Resources

Driving Questions

Use these to support students who need a little scaffolding to get them started.

1. What is the name of my business?

2. What will I serve?

3. How will I brand my business with a logo and tagline?

Check-in Questions

- What are you working on now?

- What problems have you encountered with deciding on a name/logo/menu?

- How did you solve those problems?

- What questions do you have for me?

- Why will customers choose your ice cream shop over another one?

You can find a larger collection of check-in questions in the Teacher Guide at the beginning of this packet.

Deepen the Learning Options

Use the ideas in this section to deepen the learning and increase engagement.

1. Discussion Points

What does successful mean?

Several versions of the project driving question include the word 'successful' - as in, 'create a *successful* business'.

What does it mean for a business to be successful?

Ask your learners to consider the different success criteria between for-profit and not-for-profit organizations. Consider also the different success criteria that a green, sustainable company might have compared to a multinational finance company.

Check the mini-lesson resource list for background on this topic.

How is your business unique?

Successful businesses have a USP (unique selling proposition). A business's USP is the criteria that differentiates its products from its competitors. A USP can be based on factors such as the lowest cost, the highest quality or the first-ever product of its kind.

A USP could be thought of as "what you have that competitors don't."

Ask your students to review their competitors and to develop a USP for their own ice cream shop.

Check the mini-lesson resource list for background on this topic.

2. Competition Analysis

Include the worksheets below where your learners review the menus and branding of existing ice cream shops and businesses.

3. Introduce/Encourage Professional Tools

Introduce tools such as:

- Canva for general design

- Wix Logo Maker for logo design

- Word/Google Docs for note taking and producing drafts of the menu

Ice Cream Shop Tycoon 

4. Present & Reiterate

Require learners to present their draft ideas to the class or small-group for review. Allow time for revision.

Scheduling

The more 'deepen the learning' options included, the more time you need to allow in your schedule. Similarly, developing a progress assessment tool during class will also add time.

Complete the checklist below to help you estimate the time required. Based on your knowledge of your students, estimate the number of additional class sessions you should allow in your schedule.

☐ Basic requirements, including results presentation & reflection.

____

☐ Deepen the learning discussion points   _______________________

☐ New software tools   _______________________

☐ Competition analysis   _______________________

☐ Interim draft review & reiteration   _______________________

☐ Progress assessment tool development   _______________________

Total class sessions estimated _______________________

Mini-Lesson Resources

Below you will find resources to cover most of the gaps that students are likely to encounter during this module.

Mini-Lesson	Resources
How to Name a Business	Vistaprint: https://geni.us/icecreamnaming1 USA Today: https://geni.us/icecreamnaming2 Business Name Generator: https://geni.us/icecreamnaming3
How to Start an Ice Cream Shop	DairyTechnologist.com: https://geni.us/icecreamnaming4 WikiHow.com: https://geni.us/icecreamnaming5 ShopKeep.com: https://geni.us/icecreamnaming6
How to Make Your Ice Cream Shop Unique / Plan Your Menu	Lavu.com: https://geni.us/icecreamnaming7 StartupJungle.com: https://geni.us/icecreamnaming8 (Step 5)
Designing a Logo	99Designs: https://geni.us/icecreamnaming9 Design Tools

	Canva: https://www.canva.com Wix Logo Maker: https://www.wix.com/logo/maker (Both have options to download your logo for free.)
Building a Brand	FreshSparks.com: https://geni.us/icecreamnaming10 Entrepreneur.com: https://geni.us/icecreamnaming11
What does it mean for a business to be successful?	Chron Small Business: https://geni.us/icecreamnaming12 Business News Daily: https://geni.us/icecreamnaming13
What is your USP?	Entrepreneur.com: https://geni.us/icecreamnaming14 SlideShare.net: https://geni.us/icecreamnaming15

Student Resources

See below for Included worksheets:

You will also need:

Required

Drawing materials & paper

Optional

Software tools for logo design, such as Canva, Wix Logo Maker, etc.

Student Worksheets

Competition Analysis

Complete this form for two different ice cream shops. Find pictures online or use memories from your own expe...

ICE CREAM SHOP REVIEWED: _______________

What does the name tell me about the type of ice cr... available?

How do the logo and menu work together?

What things do you like about the name, menu and l... this shop? What do you dislike?

35

My Ice Cream Shop Name

What do I already know about naming an ice cream sh...

What questions do I have about naming an ice cream s...

What issues are important when naming an ice cream sl...

Ice Cream Shop Menus Brainstorm

What do I already know about ice cream shop menus?

What issues are important when deciding on an ice cream shop menu?

What questions do I have about ice cream shop menus? What do I need to know?

37

My Ice Cream Shop Menu Ideas

What menu items will go with your name? Brainstorm... below. Identify those items that will be in your final m...

Types of Ice Cream

Different Ways of Serving

Other food and non-food items for sale

Menu Descriptions

For each of the items on your final menu, note down t... name of the item and write a description for it. Make s... your descriptions sound really enticing!

Menu Item	Description

Business Logos Analysis

Complete the forms for two well-known logos.

Name of Company	
Colors and components of the logo	
3 words that describe the 'feeling' of the logo	
How does the logo support the business?	

of Company	
and components of	
that describe the	

My Business Logo

What three words encompass the 'feel' of your busin...

What could you include in your logo to convey thos... feelings?

Create 5 possible logo designs below. Identify the ... you like best.

41

Name & Logo Reflection

Share your business name and logo with another classmate/group. Ask them what type of ice cream th... think your shop will serve.

Do their ideas match your vision?

Do their responses make you want to change anything?

Was it difficult to make the decisions involved in this module?

What was easy and what was difficult?

Which part of your work do you like the best?

42

Menu Reflection

What were two key issues you had to take into account when designing your menu?

Who will your menu appeal to? Who will it not appeal to?

What would someone who is lactose-intolerant order from your shop?

43

5. Workspace Layout Module

Module Topic

The resources in this module guide your students through designing the workspace of their ice cream shop.

End Product

- 2D or 3D layout of ice cream shop, focusing primarily on an efficient workspace layout.

Teacher Resources

Driving Question

Use this module-specific driving question to orient your students to their destination.

> How can I design the inside of my shop so I can store ingredients and products safely and prepare orders quickly?

Check-in Questions

In addition to the more general questions introduced in the Teacher Guide, ask your students:

- Have you included the appliances and utensils needed to prepare every item on your menu?

- Do you have storage for all the food and utensils you need for every item on your menu?

- Have you stepped through the preparation of your items to make sure everything is within-reach and where you need it?

- How will your layout work if you have three people working at once?

- Where will people pay and pick up their order?

Deepen the Learning Options

1. Discussion Points

What does it mean to prepare food 'safely'?
Get your learners thinking about the different aspects of safety in food preparation and delivery. Issues to consider include food contamination, knife usage, movement of heavy items, etc.

If you have two different workers making two different menu items, will they get in each other's way?
Get your students to role-play food preparation in their ice cream shop. You can use masking tape on the floor to map out the actual size and layout of the ice cream shop.

Ice Cream Shop Tycoon 

What problems do your students encounter as they try and move around the ice cream shop to prepare the different menu items? Is a redesign required?

What if there are three people working in the shop? How will your students split their roles in this workspace for the best efficiency?

How long do your menu items take to prepare? How many people can you serve per hour?
Get your learners to consider how long it takes them to prepare each menu item. Again, getting them to step through the actual process can show up issues with the workspace layout or with the menu.

Do your students need to reconsider their menu in light of their findings? Or do they need to reconsider the workspace design?

2. Introduce/Encourage Professional Tools

For more challenge, consider introducing easy-to-use 3-D and 2-D design software such as:

- Kitchen Planner

- Room Sketcher

See the Mini-lessons Resource section for more information.

3. Build a 3-D Model

If you want to prioritise learning standards from art or design, suggest your learners build scaled 3-D models of their shop. These will be a great addition if your culminating event is an ice cream shop fair.

4. Use Real-World Data

Increase the reality of the project by requiring learners to search online for appliance dimensions and capabilities.

5. Present & Reiterate

Require learners to present their draft ideas to the class or peers for review. Allow time for revision. This option becomes redundant if learners have already done tape-on-the-floor mock-ups.

Scheduling

This module can be completed in as little as one to two class periods, where students brainstorm their ideas and come up with a first draft of the layout.

Complete the checklist below to determine a more realistic time-frame that suits your students' learning needs.

☐ Basic requirements, including results presentation & reflection.

____

☐ Deepen the learning discussion points   _______________________

☐ Build a 3-D model   _______________________

☐ New software tools   _______________________

☐ Interim draft review & reiteration   _______________________

☐ Use real-world data   _______________________

☐ Progress assessment tool development   _______________________

Total Class sessions estimated _______________________

Mini-Lesson Resources

Below you will find resources to cover most of the gaps that students are likely to encounter during this module.

Mini-Lesson	Resources
Kitchen Design Tools	KitchenPlanner.net: https://geni.us/icecreaminterior1 RoomSketcher.com: https://geni.us/icecreaminterior2
Things to consider when designing a kitchen	Ice cream shop-specific Resources: IceCreamProfits.com: https://geni.us/icecreaminterior3 KalScoops.com: https://geni.us/icecreaminterior4 ParExcellenceMagazine.com: https://geni.us/icecreaminterior5 YouTube: https://geni.us/icecreaminterior6 More General Resources: IdealHome.co.uk: https://geni.us/icecreaminterior7 Better Homes & Gardens: https://geni.us/icecreaminterior8

Finding equipment prices and dimensions	WebstaurantStore.com: https://geni.us/icecreaminterior9 WebstaurantStore.com: https://geni.us/icecreaminterior10

Student Resources

See below for Included worksheets:

You will also need:

Required

Drawing materials & paper. Scissors & glue.

Optional

Access to free online design software such as Kitchen Planner and Room Sketcher.

NOTE: If your students are developing independent learning skills, consider using the student worksheets as a reference for you to prompt, question and guide your students' thinking rather than something they need to fill in. Scaffolding them to come up with the worksheet questions themselves will generate much more powerful learning.

Student Worksheets

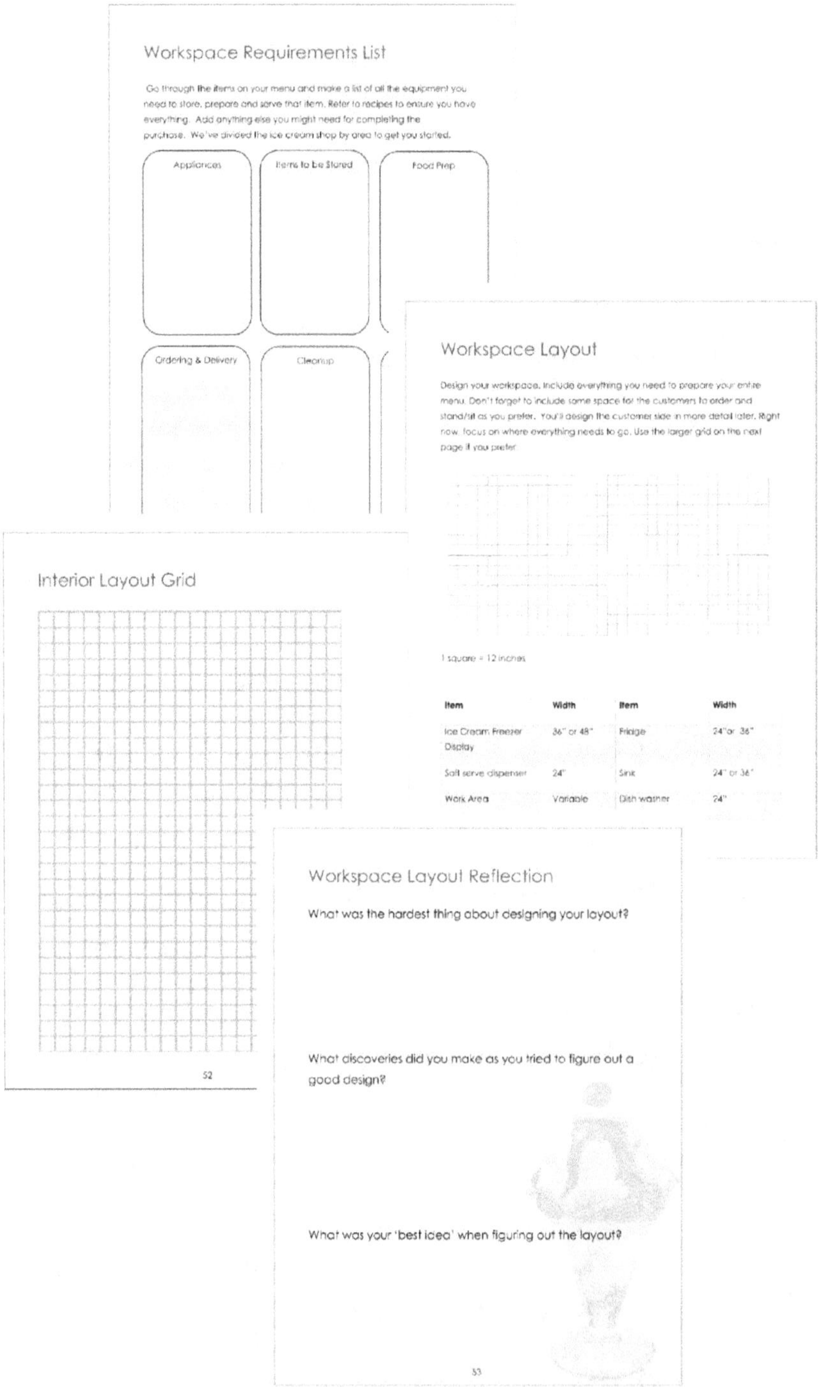

Workspace Requirements List

Go through the items on your menu and make a list of all the equipment you need to store, prepare and serve that item. Refer to recipes to ensure you have everything. Add anything else you might need for completing the purchase. We've divided the ice cream shop by area to get you started.

Appliances	Items to be Stored	Food Prep

Ordering & Delivery	Cleanup	

Workspace Layout

Design your workspace. Include everything you need to prepare your entire menu. Don't forget to include some space for the customers to order and stand/sit as you prefer. You'll design the customer side in more detail later. Right now, focus on where everything needs to go. Use the larger grid on the next page if you prefer.

1 square = 12 inches

Item	Width	Item	Width
Ice Cream Freezer Display	36" or 48"	Fridge	24" or 36"
Soft serve dispenser	24"	Sink	24" or 36"
Work Area	Variable	Dish washer	24"

Interior Layout Grid

52

Workspace Layout Reflection

What was the hardest thing about designing your layout?

What discoveries did you make as you tried to figure out a good design?

What was your 'best idea' when figuring out the layout?

53

6. Customer Experience Module

Module Topic

In this module your students consider their customer's experience in their shop. This includes the exterior appearance of the shop, the visible menus, areas for ordering, food pick-up and sitting/standing.

End Product

By the end of this module, your learners will have:

- Designed visual appearance of the interior and exterior of their ice cream shop,

- Designed a visibly appealing menu.

- Identified any other engaging features they wish to include in the customer experience.

Teacher Resources

Driving Question

Use this module-specific driving question to orient your students to their destination.

> What will the buying experience be for my customers? (What will they see, hear, smell, do as they approach, enter and make a purchase?)

Check-in Questions

In addition to the more general questions introduced in the Teacher Guide, ask your students:

- How easy is it for your customers to see your menu? How big will it be?

- Is it clear where your customers should order and pickup their ice cream?

- Will your interior and exterior design for customers work if there is a big line-up?

- If someone sees your ice cream shop from a block away, will they immediately know what type of food you sell?

Deepen the Learning Options

1. Discussion Points

What feeling do you want your customers to have about your ice cream shop? How does your exterior experience contribute to or take away from that goal?
> Get your learners thinking about setting your customer's expectations by providing an exterior experience that guides them to that expectation.

How is your USP communicated?
> If you analyzed your USP (unique selling proposition) in the module on naming, describe how you convey your USP though the exterior and interior of your shop.

2. Introduce/Encourage Professional Tools

For more challenge, consider introducing easy-to-use design software such as Canva.

3. Finish the 3-D Model

If your students previously built a 3-D model, encourage them to complete it by showing the customer experience.

4. Present & Reiterate

Require learners to present their draft ideas to the class or peers for review. Allow time for revision.

Scheduling

Complete the checklist below to help you estimate the time required. Based on your knowledge of your students, estimate the number of additional class sessions you should allow in your schedule.

☐ Basic requirements, including results presentation & reflection.

____

☐ Deepen the learning discussion points   ____________________

☐ Complete a 3-D model   ____________________

☐ New software tools   ____________________

☐ Interim draft review & reiteration   ____________________

☐ Progress assessment tool development   ____________________

Total Class sessions estimated ____________________

Mini-Lesson Resources

Below you will find resources to cover most of the gaps that students are likely to encounter during this module.

Mini-Lesson	Resources
Ice Cream Shop /Restaurant Customer Experience Design	Posist.com: https://geni.us/icecreamcustomer1 CustomerService.ae: https://geni.us/icecreamcustomer2
Software Tools for Design	Canva (easier for quick learning) https://pixlr.com/x/
Designing the appearance of your menu	Canva.com: https://geni.us/icecreamcustomer3 DSMenu.com: https://geni.us/icecreamcustomer4

Student Resources

See below for Included worksheets:

You will also need:

Required

Drawing materials & paper

Optional

Software tools for shop and menu design, such as Canva, Pixlr.

Student Worksheets

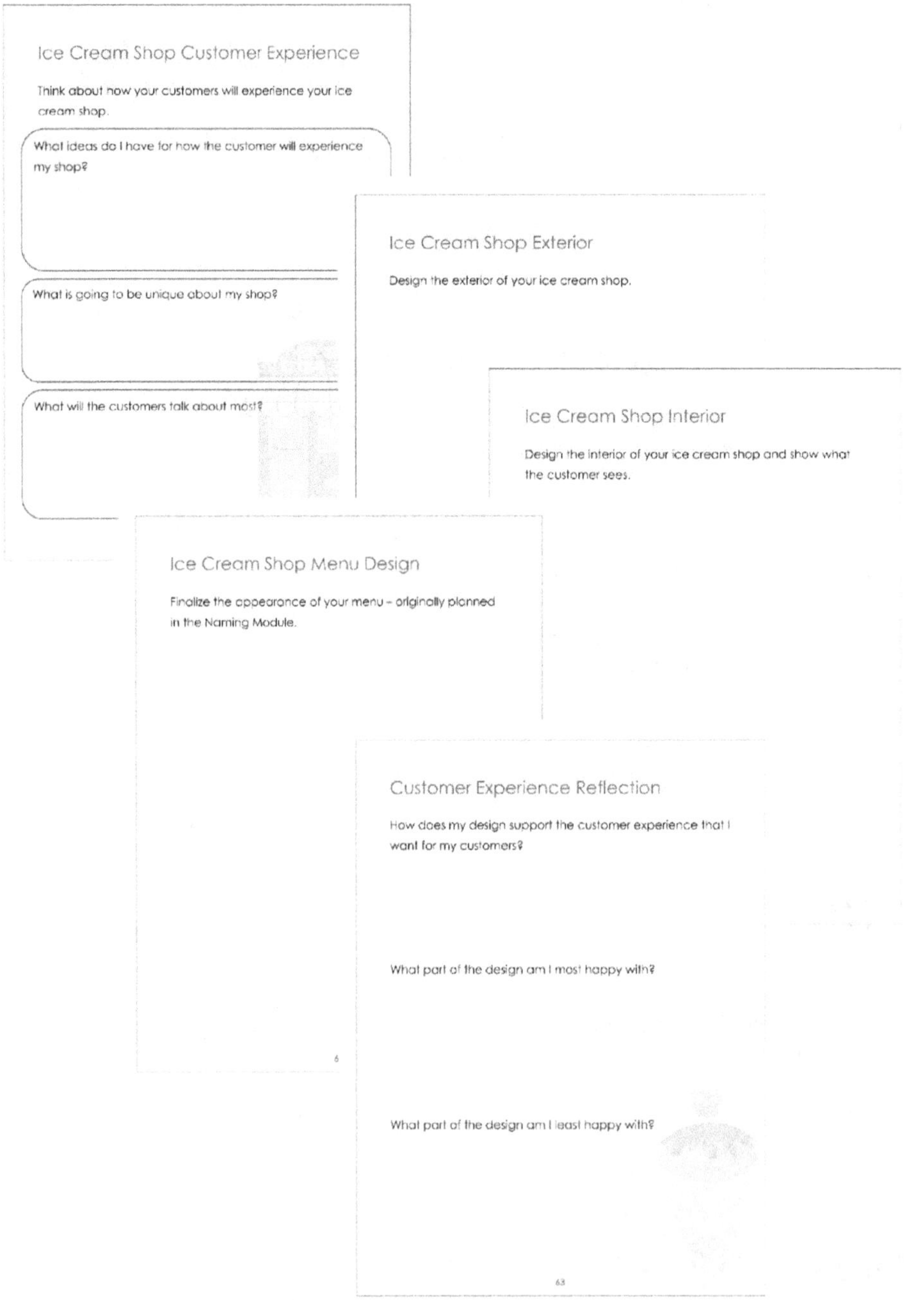

Ice Cream Shop Customer Experience

Think about how your customers will experience your ice cream shop.

What ideas do I have for how the customer will experience my shop?

What is going to be unique about my shop?

What will the customers talk about most?

Ice Cream Shop Exterior

Design the exterior of your ice cream shop.

Ice Cream Shop Interior

Design the interior of your ice cream shop and show what the customer sees.

Ice Cream Shop Menu Design

Finalize the appearance of your menu – originally planned in the Naming Module.

Customer Experience Reflection

How does my design support the customer experience that I want for my customers?

What part of the design am I most happy with?

What part of the design am I least happy with?

7. Pricing and Costs Module

Module Topic

In this module students investigate how much it costs to start an ice cream shop and how to calculate the unit cost of a menu item. They then use industry metrics to price the menu item.

End Product

By the end of this module, your learners will have a start-up cost and will have priced at least one of their menu items in a way that allows their business to be profitable.

Teacher Resources

Driving Questions

How much will it cost to start my business?

What will my ingredients cost and how should I price my menu?

   Ice Cream Shop Tycoon 

Check-in Questions

In addition to the more general questions introduced in the Teacher Guide, ask your students:

- Start-up costs: Have you budgeted for everything in your interior layout?

- Start-up costs: Have you budgeted for everything on your exterior?

- Start-up costs: Have you been surprised by anything?

- Menu pricing: What's your biggest challenge right now in determining the cost of this menu item?

- Menu pricing: Does your final menu price suit your target audience?

Deepen the Learning

1. Discussion Points

What other costs do you have to operate your business, besides the cost of food?
Get your learners thinking about the costs involved in running a business. These will include electricity, gas, wages, credit card fees, etc.

If your budget was 80% of your estimated start-up costs, what would you change in order to come in under budget?
Business owners frequently have to make compromises because of the realities of the world. Get your students thinking about how they can reduce costs.

2. Use Real-World Data

Get your students to investigate how the restaurant/ice cream shop
industry prices menu items. Require them to provide reasoning for the
method they choose.

3. Provide a Challenge & Reiterate

In the real world, business owners get nasty surprises. Require learners to
present their start-up costs and pricing to the class or peers for review.
Next, provide each group with a different challenge, ask them for a quick
solution and then allow time for revision.

For example, reduce the budgets for the start-up costs, put a maximum
price on a menu item which then requires a rethink. Tell another group
that a certain ingredient actually costs twice as much because of a
shortage. Generally, put your students on the spot and make them think.

Scheduling

Complete the checklist below to help you estimate the time required. Based on
your knowledge of your students, estimate the number of additional class
sessions you should allow in your schedule.

☐ Basic requirements, including results presentation & reflection.

____

☐ Deepen the learning discussion points   ____________________

☐ Using real world data   ____________________

☐ Adding the additional challenge   ____________________

☐ Progress assessment tool development   ____________________

Total class sessions estimated ______________________

Mini-Lesson Resources

Below you will find resources to cover most of the gaps that students are likely to encounter during this module.

Mini-Lesson	Resources
Ice Cream Shop Equipment Prices	WebstaurantStore.com: https://geni.us/icecreampricing1 WebstaurantStore.com: https://geni.us/icecreampricing2
Ingredient Prices	Introduce students to online grocery shopping sites/apps for quick access to current food prices.
Ice Cream Shop Start-up & Operating Costs	Alcas.us: https://geni.us/icecreampricing3

Ice Cream Shop/Restaurant Menu Pricing	ChronSmall Business: https://geni.us/icecreampricing4 WebstaurantStore.com: https://geni.us/icecreampricing5 rMagazine.com: https://geni.us/icecreampricing6

Student Resources

See below for Included worksheets:

You will also need:

Required

> Drawing materials & paper

> A means of accessing ice cream shop equipment prices.

> A means of accessing food prices.

Optional

> Calculator for adding costs and calculating unit costs

Student Worksheets

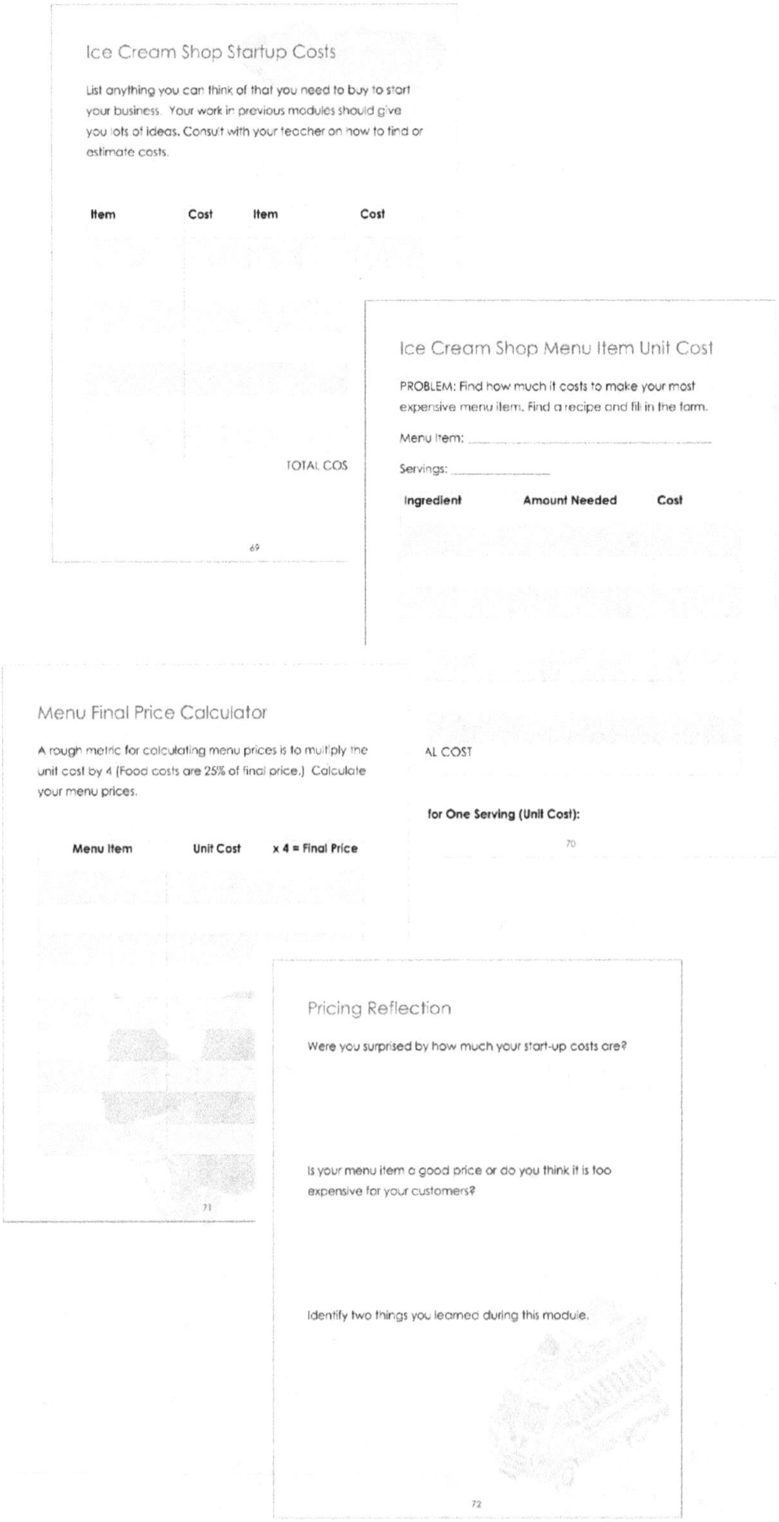

Ice Cream Shop Startup Costs

List anything you can think of that you need to buy to start your business. Your work in previous modules should give you lots of ideas. Consult with your teacher on how to find or estimate costs.

Item	Cost	Item	Cost

TOTAL COS

69

Ice Cream Shop Menu Item Unit Cost

PROBLEM: Find how much it costs to make your most expensive menu item. Find a recipe and fill in the form.

Menu Item: _______________________________

Servings: _______________

Ingredient	Amount Needed	Cost

Menu Final Price Calculator

A rough metric for calculating menu prices is to multiply the unit cost by 4 (Food costs are 25% of final price.) Calculate your menu prices.

Menu Item	Unit Cost	x 4 = Final Price

AL COST

for One Serving (Unit Cost):

70

71

Pricing Reflection

Were you surprised by how much your start-up costs are?

Is your menu item a good price or do you think it is too expensive for your customers?

Identify two things you learned during this module.

72

8. Marketing Module

Module Topic

In this module students learn how to make their audience aware of their business.

End Product

Depending on the grade-level of your students and your learning goals, your students will produce one or more of the following:

- Instagram Post

- Flyer

- Business Website

Ice Cream Shop Tycoon

Teacher Resources

Driving Question

How will my customers hear about and find information about my business?

Check-in Questions

In addition to the more general questions introduced in the Teacher Guide, ask your students:

- Does your Instagram post reflect your brand?

- What is your goal with this Instagram post?

- What is the number one thing your customers need to know from your marketing & advertising?

- Who is your ideal customer and how will he/she hear about your ice cream shop?

- What information will your customer need from the flyer? Have you included all that information in an easy to read way?

Deepen the Learning

1. Discussion Points

Who is your ideal customer? Be very explicit when describing who they are, what they do, etc. Why are they your ideal customer?

Identifying your key customer is vital for knowing how to reach them cost-effectively.   Are your customers going to be office workers on a lunch break? Or are they families out on a Sunday afternoon?   Are you aiming for a young trendy crowd who wants to try innovative ice cream flavors? Or are you aiming at people who are looking for their favorites?

What are the 3 effective ways to get information about your business in front of your ideal customer? What would be a bad way to market your shop to this group of people?
Different groups of people are marketed to in different ways. Young people are found on Instagram. Older people are on Facebook. Get your learners to think of traditional or innovative ways to reach their specific demographic.

How will you measure whether your marketing strategies are successful?
Marketing your business takes time and/or money. How will you measure each marketing strategy to determine whether it is making a difference?

2. Introduce/Encourage Professional Tools

For more challenge, consider introducing easy-to-use design software such as Canva and website builders such as Wix.

Designing even a simple website may add significant time, but it is an excellent skill to learn.

 Ice Cream Shop Tycoon 

3. Present & Reiterate

> Require learners to present their draft ideas to the class or peers for review.
> Allow time for revision.

Scheduling

Complete the checklist below to help you estimate the time required. Based on your knowledge of your students, estimate the number of additional class sessions you should allow in your schedule.

☐ Basic requirements, including results presentation & reflection.

____

☐ Deepen the learning discussion points   ____________________

☐ Using/Learning software tools   ____________________

☐ Progress assessment tool development   ____________________

Total class sessions estimated ____________________

Mini-Lesson Resources

Below you will find resources to cover most of the gaps that students are likely to encounter during this module.

Mini-Lesson	Resources
Wix or Wordpress	www.wix.com www.wordpress.com
Marketing an Ice cream shop with Instagram	Entrepreneur.com: https://geni.us/icecreammarketing1 WebstaurantStore.com: https://geni.us/icecreammarketing2
Designing a Simple Business Website Design Inspiration	Wix.com: https://geni.us/icecreammarketing3 TripWireMagazine.com: https://geni.us/icecreammarketing4

Student Resources

See below for Included worksheets:

You will also need:

Required

Drawing materials & paper

Optional

Access to flyer design software such as Canva.

Access to website building software such as Wix or Wordpress.

Student Worksheets

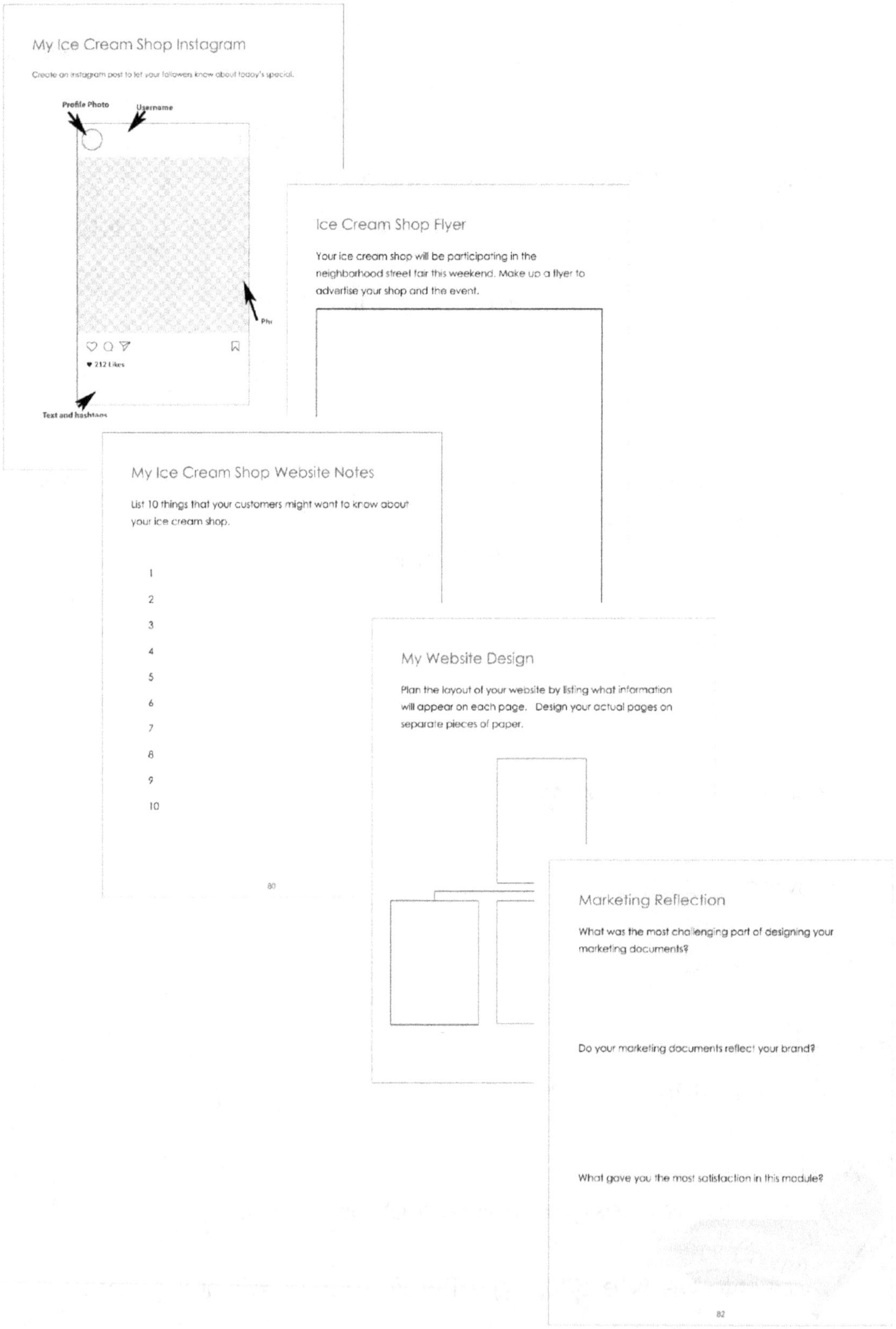
My Ice Cream Shop Instagram
Create an Instagram post to let your followers know about today's special.
Profile Photo
Username
212 Likes
Text and hashtags
Ice Cream Shop Flyer
Your ice cream shop will be participating in the neighborhood street fair this weekend. Make up a flyer to advertise your shop and the event.
My Ice Cream Shop Website Notes
List 10 things that your customers might want to know about your ice cream shop.
1
2
3
4
5
6
7
8
9
10
80
My Website Design
Plan the layout of your website by listing what information will appear on each page. Design your actual pages on separate pieces of paper.
Marketing Reflection
What was the most challenging part of designing your marketing documents?
Do your marketing documents reflect your brand?
What gave you the most satisfaction in this module?
82

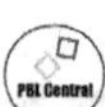

9. Culminating Event Module

Your students have come so far! It's time to let them demonstrate their progress with an awesome final event.

In this module you will find ideas and resources for conducting a memorable and engaging culminating event.

The purpose of the culminating event is to showcase your students' work to an audience, whether that be student peers, other classes or staff, parents or community members.

Below you will suggestions for three alternate culminating events. The best choice for your students will depend on the driving question you chose.

Your options include:

- Ice Cream Shop Fair

- Ice Cream Shop Field Trip

- Business Plan Presentation

Ice Cream Shop Tycoon

Ice Cream Shop Fair

Hold an ice cream shop fair in your classroom. Let your students display their ice cream shop materials for an audience of classmates, peers, or parents. The audience can be given a budget to spend at the ice cream shop.

In this scenario, each audience member is given a spending form and a budget. They wander the ice cream shop fair and spend their budget ordering ice creams and talking to the ice cream shop vendors. The form is used to keep track of what they have spent and to include comments about each shop they patronise.

Ice cream shop vendors keep track of what is ordered from their shop on their order form.

If this is an in-class experience, give the members of each shop 10 minutes to close their shop and spend at other shops. (You may want to include this even if you have an out-of-class audience.)

At the end of the event, retrieve the comment forms from the audience and ask the shop owners to add up their sales. While they are doing this, find 1-2 awesome comments for each shop. When you have everyone's attention, read out the comments to the audience.

If you wish to introduce a competitive element, you could have awards for most sales, most popular single item (number of orders), most orders at a shop, etc.

And don't forget to serve some ice cream at the end!

Ice Cream Shop Field Trip

If you haven't already found a reason to visit some ice cream shops during the project, the culminating day is an excellent opportunity.

Your field trip can be as simple as visiting a variety of ice cream shops to sample the food, or if you contact the ice cream shop owners in advance, you may be able to arrange for a 5-minute question and answer session with the owner or manager.

Alternatively, you can use the opportunity for your learners to evaluate the ice cream shop experience from a customer's perspective. At the end of this section, you will find a sample ice cream shop review form - or as an even better option, your class can design one as part of the project.

Business Plan Presentation

For those classes that have produced something closer to a real business plan, an excellent culminating event is to invite an ice cream shop entrepreneur or small-business investor or loans manager to class to listen to the students' business presentations.

We recommend providing any audience member with a 1-page guide to evaluating/commenting on the student's work. We provide a sample Welcome/Thank-You form below.

Scheduling

You may need to schedule some additional class time for your students to create the final versions of their end products - if they have not already done so as part of each module.

Last Comments

Have a blast with the final event. Make sure your students recognize how much they have learned along the way – not just in content but in learning skills as well.

Student Worksheets

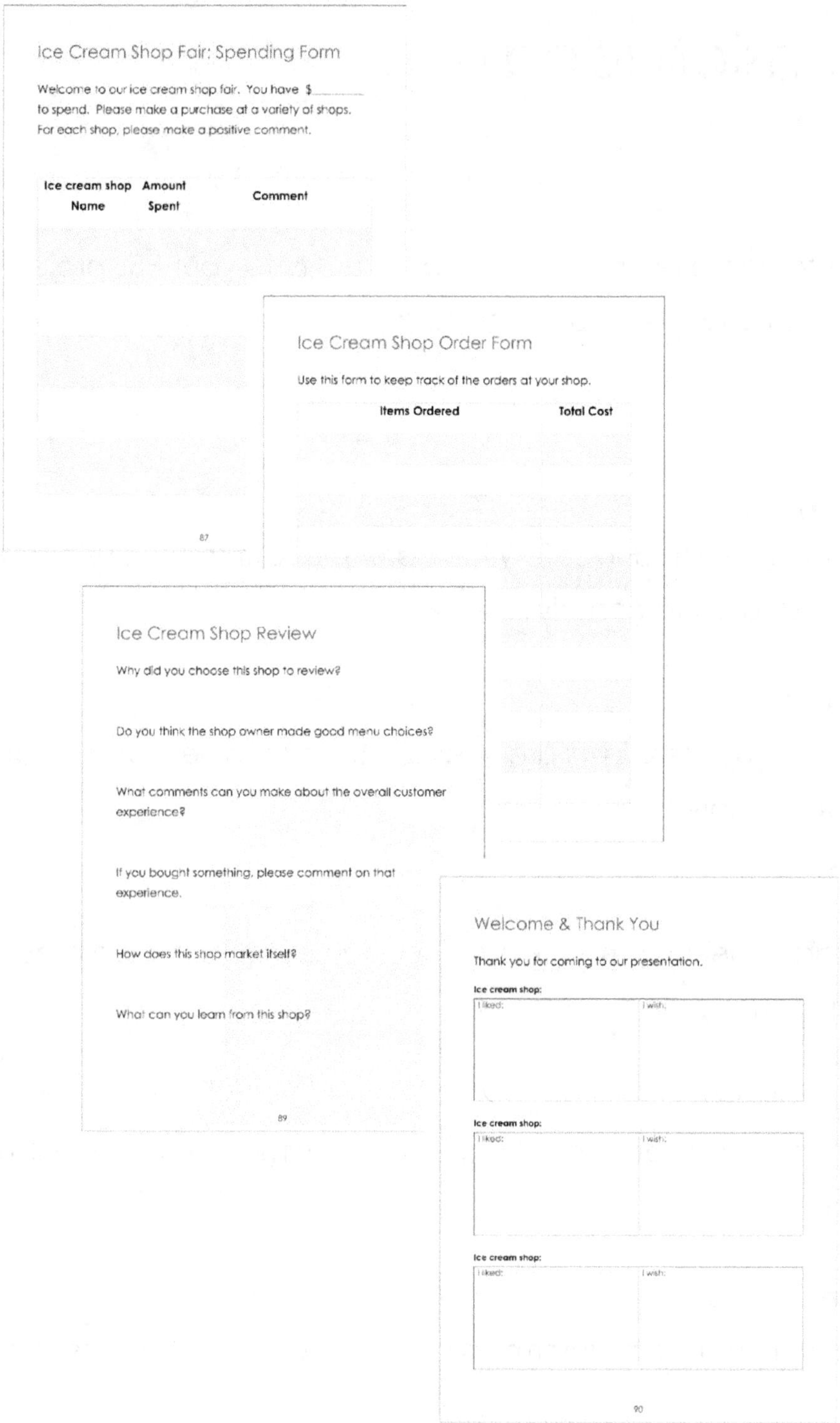

Ice Cream Shop Fair: Spending Form

Welcome to our ice cream shop fair. You have $ _________
to spend. Please make a purchase at a variety of shops.
For each shop, please make a positive comment.

Ice cream shop Name	Amount Spent	Comment

87

Ice Cream Shop Order Form

Use this form to keep track of the orders at your shop.

Items Ordered	Total Cost

Ice Cream Shop Review

Why did you choose this shop to review?

Do you think the shop owner made good menu choices?

What comments can you make about the overall customer experience?

If you bought something, please comment on that experience.

How does this shop market itself?

What can you learn from this shop?

89

Welcome & Thank You

Thank you for coming to our presentation.

Ice cream shop:

I liked:	I wish:

Ice cream shop:

I liked:	I wish:

Ice cream shop:

I liked:	I wish:

90

10. Extension Ideas

Do you want to add even more depth and reality to your PBL project? Below we include additional ideas for older students.

Health & Safety

> What local health and safety laws are relevant to my business and what do I need to do to comply?

Permits and Laws

> What local business laws are relevant to my business and what do I need to do to comply?

Diversifying

> What are other income streams that can expand my ice cream shop income?

Financial Projections

> How can I make realistic estimates for how much money I will make in the first year?

Business Plan

> How can I present my information in a way that will impress a potential investor?

11. Learning Standards

The ice cream shop project can encompass a huge variety of learning standards across a range of grades. Below you will find a list of non-grade-specific standards that you can map to your own state requirements.

Language Arts

- Comprehend and connect (reading, listening, viewing)

- Access information and ideas for diverse purposes and from a variety of sources and evaluate their relevance, accuracy, and reliability

- Apply appropriate strategies to comprehend written, oral, and visual texts, guide inquiry, and extend thinking

  Synthesize ideas from a variety of sources to build understanding
- Recognize and appreciate how different features, forms, and genres of texts reflect different purposes, audiences, and messages

- Think critically, creatively, and reflectively to explore ideas within, between, and beyond texts

- Recognize and identify the role of personal, social, and cultural contexts, values, and perspectives in texts

- Recognize how language constructs personal, social, and cultural identity

- Construct meaningful personal connections between self, text, and world

- Respond to text in personal, creative, and critical ways

- Create and communicate (writing, speaking, representing)

- Exchange ideas and viewpoints to build shared understanding and extend thinking

- Use writing and design processes to plan, develop, and create engaging and meaningful literary and informational texts for a variety of purposes and audiences

- Assess and refine texts to improve their clarity, effectiveness, and impact according to purpose, audience, and message

- Use an increasing repertoire of conventions of spelling, grammar, and punctuation

- Use and experiment with oral storytelling processes

- Select and use appropriate features, forms, and genres according to audience, purpose, and message

- Transform ideas and information to create original texts.

Applied Design

Understanding context

- Empathize with potential users to find issues and uncover needs and potential design opportunities

Defining

- ·Choose a design opportunity

- Identify key features or potential users and their requirements

- Identify criteria for success and any constraints

Ideating

- Generate potential ideas and add to others' ideas

- Screen ideas against criteria and constraints

- Evaluate personal, social, and environmental impacts and ethical considerations

- Choose an idea to pursue

Prototyping

- Identify and use sources of information

- Develop a plan that identifies key stages and resources

- Explore and test a variety of materials for effective use

- Construct a first version of the product or a prototype, as appropriate, making changes to tools, materials, and procedures as needed

- Record iterations of prototyping

Testing

- Test the first version of the product or the prototype

- Gather peer and/or user and/or expert feedback and inspiration

- Make changes, troubleshoot, and test again

Making

- Identify and use appropriate tools, technologies, and materials for production

- Make a plan for production that includes key stages, and carry it out, making changes as needed

- ·Use materials in ways that minimize waste

Sharing

- Decide on how and with whom to share their product

Ice Cream Shop Tycoon 

- Demonstrate their product and describe their process, using appropriate terminology and providing reasons for their selected solution and modifications

- Evaluate their product against their criteria and explain how it contributes to the individual, family, community, and/or environment

- Reflect on their design thinking and processes, and evaluate their ability to work effectively both as individuals and collaboratively in a group, including their ability to share and maintain an efficient cooperative work space

- Identify new design issues

Applied Skills

- Demonstrate an awareness of precautionary and emergency safety procedures in both physical and digital environments

- Identify and evaluate the skills and skill levels needed, individually or as a group, in relation to a specific task, and develop them as needed

Applied Technologies

- Select, and as needed learn about, appropriate tools and technologies to extend their capability to complete a task

- Identify the personal, social, and environmental impacts, including unintended negative consequences, of the choices they make about technology use

- Identify how the land, natural resources, and culture influence the development and use of tools and technologies

Career Education

- Apply a variety of research skills to expand their knowledge of diverse career possibilities and understand career clusters

- Recognize the impact of personal public identity in the world of work

- Demonstrate respect, collaboration, and inclusivity in working with others to solve problems

- Recognize and explore diverse perspectives on how work contributes to our community and society

- Demonstrate safety skills and appreciate the importance of workplace safety

- Set and achieve realistic learning goals with perseverance and resilience

- Explore volunteer and other new learning experiences that stimulate entrepreneurial and innovative thinking

- Apply decision-making strategies to a life, work or community problem and adjust the strategies to adapt to new situations

Social Studies

- Use Social Studies inquiry processes and skills to ask questions; gather, interpret, and analyze ideas; and communicate findings and decisions

- Assess the significance of people, places, events, or developments at particular times and places (significance)

- Identify what the creators of accounts, narratives, maps, or texts have determined is significant (significance)

- Assess the credibility of multiple sources and the adequacy of evidence used to justify conclusions (evidence)

Math

Reasoning and analyzing

- Use reasoning and logic to explore, analyze, and apply mathematical ideas

- Estimate reasonably

Ice Cream Shop Tycoon 

- Demonstrate and apply mental math strategies

- Model mathematics in contextualized experiences

Understanding and solving

- Engage in problem-solving experiences

- Develop, demonstrate, and apply mathematical understanding through play, inquiry, and problem solving

- Visualize to explore mathematical concepts

Communicating and representing

- Use mathematical vocabulary and language to contribute to mathematical discussions

- Explain and justify mathematical ideas and decisions

- Communicate mathematical thinking in many ways

- Represent mathematical ideas in concrete, pictorial, and symbolic forms

Connecting and reflecting

- Reflect on mathematical thinking

- Connect mathematical concepts to each other and to other areas and personal interests

- Use mathematical arguments to support personal choices

Art

Exploring and creating

- Intentionally select and apply materials, movements, technologies, environments, tools, and techniques by combining and arranging artistic elements, processes, and principles in art making

- Create artistic works collaboratively and as an individual using ideas inspired by imagination, inquiry, experimentation, and purposeful play

- Demonstrate an understanding and appreciation of personal, social, cultural, historical, and environmental contexts in relation to the arts

Reasoning and reflecting

- Describe, interpret and evaluate how artists (dancers, actors, musicians, and visual artists) use processes, materials, movements, technologies, tools, techniques, and environments to create and communicate ideas

- Develop, refine ideas, and critically appraise ideas, processes, and technical skills in a variety of art forms to improve the quality of artistic creations

- Reflect on works of art and creative processes to understand artists motivations and meanings

- Interpret works of art using knowledge and skills from various areas of learning

- Respond to works of art using one's knowledge of the world

Communicating and documenting

- Adapt learned skills, understandings, and processes for use in new contexts and for different purposes and audiences

- Interpret and communicate ideas using symbols and elements to express meaning through the arts

- Take creative risks to express feelings, ideas, and experiences

     Ice Cream Shop Tycoon   

12. Printable Worksheets

In this section you will find all the worksheets for the project, easily accessible for printing.

Project Planning Worksheet

Project Name:

Driving Question:

Launch Event:

Culminating Event:

Modules to Include + Schedule (approx. # of classes or completion date)

- ☐ Launch Event   ____________________

- ☐ Naming, Branding & Menu   ____________________

- ☐ Workspace Layout   ____________________

- ☐ Customer Experience   ____________________

- ☐ Pricing & Costing   ____________________

- ☐ Marketing   ____________________

- ☐ Culminating Event   ____________________

Resource Sources:

Assessment:

My Driving Question is:

What Will I Do/Make/Decide When Planning My Ice Cream Shop?

My Driving Question is:

What Questions Do I Have?

71

My Driving Question is:

What Do I Need to Know?

Competition Analysis

Complete this form for two different ice cream shops. Find pictures online or use memories from your own experiences.

ICE CREAM SHOP REVIEWED:_______________________________

What does the name tell me about the type of ice cream available?

How do the logo and menu work together?

What things do you like about the name, menu and logo of this shop? What do you dislike?

My Ice Cream Shop Name

What do I already know about naming an ice cream shop?

What questions do I have about naming an ice cream shop?

What issues are important when naming an ice cream shop?

What are some ideas I have for my name?

My Business Name:

Ice Cream Shop Menus Brainstorm

What do I already know about ice cream shop menus?

What issues are important when deciding on an ice cream shop menu?

What questions do I have about ice cream shop menus? What do I need to know?

My Ice Cream Shop Menu Ideas

What menu items will go with your name? Brainstorm ideas below. Identify those items that will be in your final menu.

Types of Ice Cream

Different Ways of Serving

Other food and non-food items for sale

Menu Descriptions

For each of the items on your final menu, note down the
name of the item and write a description for it. Make sure
your descriptions sound really enticing!

Menu Item	Description

Business Logos Analysis

Complete the forms for two well-known logos.

Name of Company	
Colors and components of the logo	
3 words that describe the 'feeling' of the logo	
How does the logo support the business?	

Name of Company	
Colors and components of the logo	
3 words that describe the 'feeling' of the logo	
How does the logo support the business?	

My Business Logo

What three words encompass the 'feel' of your business?

What could you include in your logo to convey those feelings?

Create 5 possible logo designs below. Identify the one you like best.

Name & Logo Reflection

Share your business name and logo with another classmate/group. Ask them what type of ice cream they think your shop will serve.

Do their ideas match your vision?

Do their responses make you want to change anything?

Was it difficult to make the decisions involved in this module?

What was easy and what was difficult?

Which part of your work do you like the best?

Menu Reflection

What were two key issues you had to take into account when designing your menu?

Who will your menu appeal to? Who will it not appeal to?

What would someone who is lactose-intolerant order from your shop?

Workspace Requirements List

Go through the items on your menu and make a list of all the equipment you need to store, prepare and serve that item. Refer to recipes to ensure you have everything. Add anything else you might need for completing the purchase. We've divided the ice cream shop by area to get you started.

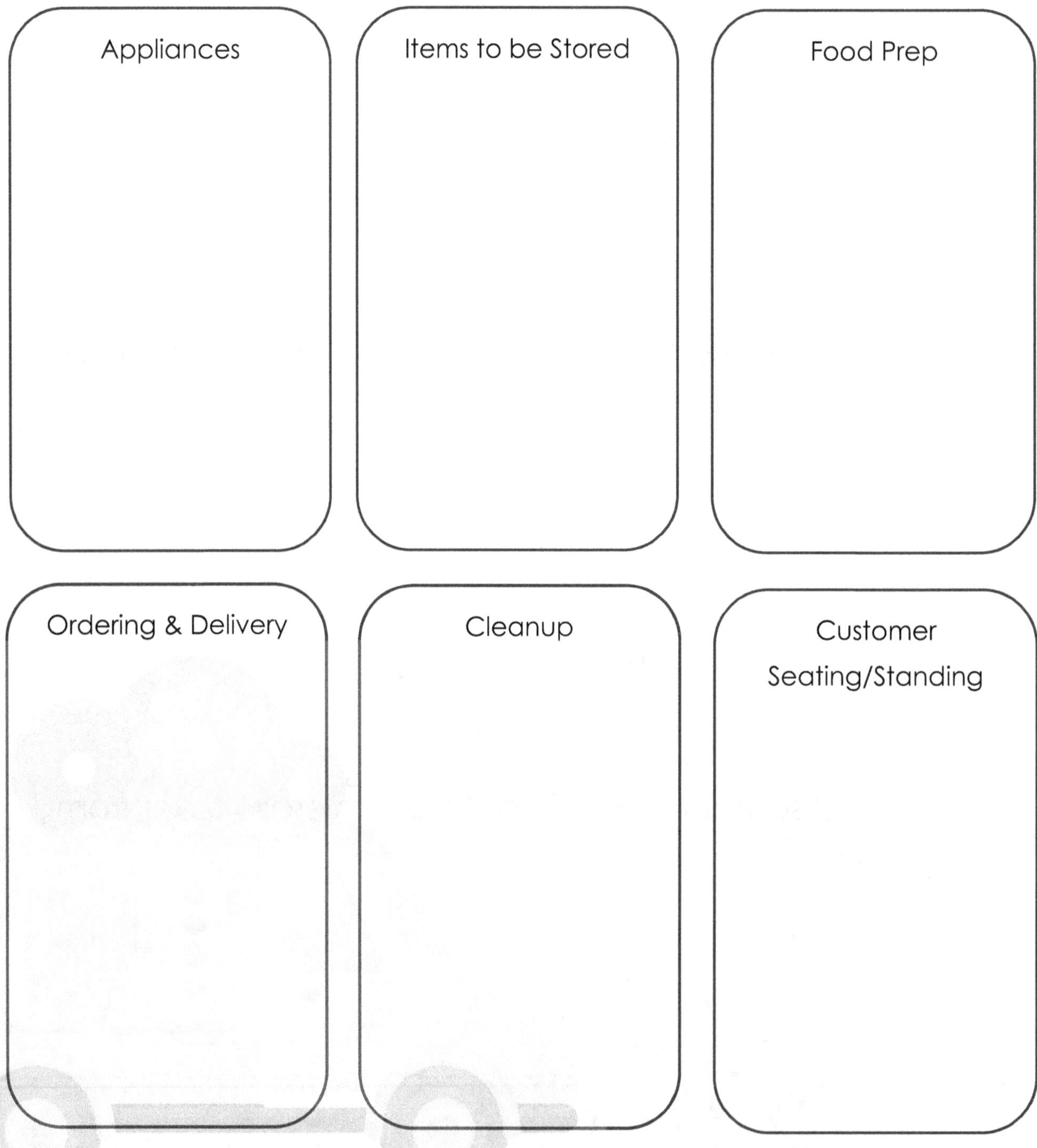

Workspace Layout

Design your workspace. Include everything you need to prepare your entire menu. Don't forget to include some space for the customers to order and stand/sit as you prefer. You'll design the customer side in more detail later. Right now, focus on where everything needs to go. Use the larger grid on the next page if you prefer.

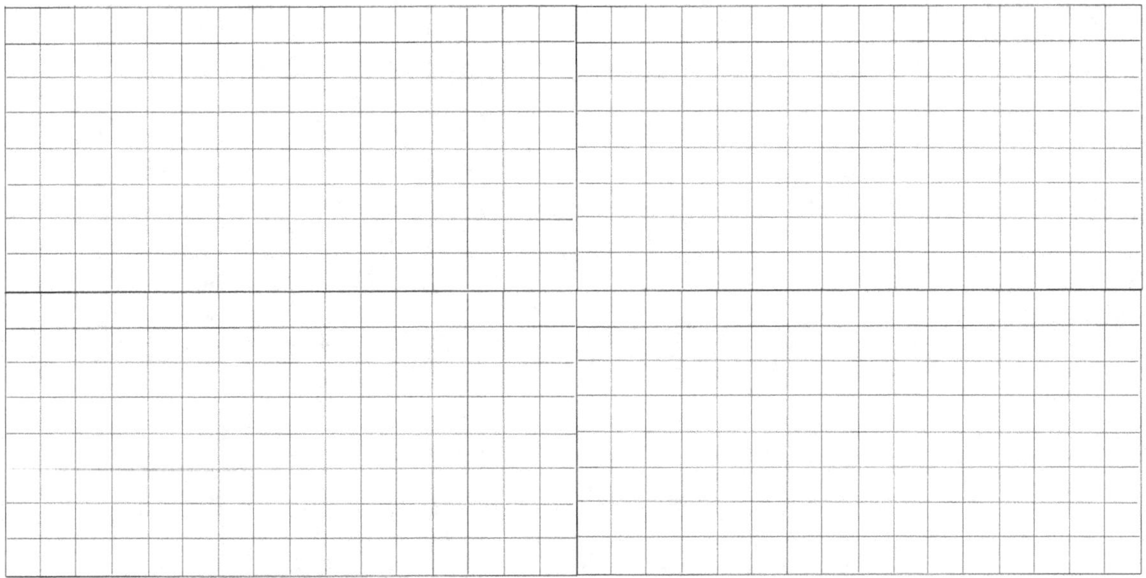

1 square = 12 inches

Item	Width	Item	Width
Ice Cream Freezer Display	36" or 48"	Fridge	24"or 36"
Soft serve dispenser	24"	Sink	24" or 36"
Work Area	Variable	Dish washer	24"

Interior Layout Grid

Workspace Layout Reflection

What was the hardest thing about designing your layout?

What discoveries did you make as you tried to figure out a good design?

What was your 'best idea' when figuring out the layout?

Ice Cream Shop Customer Experience

Think about how your customers will experience your ice cream shop.

What ideas do I have for how the customer will experience my shop?

What is going to be unique about my shop?

What will the customers talk about most?

Ice Cream Shop Exterior

Design the exterior of your ice cream shop.

Ice Cream Shop Interior

Design the interior of your ice cream shop and show what the customer sees.

Ice Cream Shop Menu Design

Finalize the appearance of your menu – originally planned in the Naming Module.

Customer Experience Reflection

How does my design support the customer experience that I want for my customers?

What part of the design am I most happy with?

What part of the design am I least happy with?

Ice Cream Shop Startup Costs

List anything you can think of that you need to buy to start your business. Your work in previous modules should give you lots of ideas. Consult with your teacher on how to find or estimate costs.

Item	Cost	Item	Cost
		TOTAL COST	

Ice Cream Shop Menu Item Unit Cost

PROBLEM: Find how much it costs to make your most expensive menu item. Find a recipe and fill in the form.

Menu Item: ____

Servings: _______________

Ingredient	Amount Needed	Cost
TOTAL COST		

Cost for One Serving (Unit Cost):

Menu Final Price Calculator

A rough metric for calculating menu prices is to multiply the unit cost by 4 (Food costs are 25% of final price.) Calculate your menu prices.

Menu Item	Unit Cost	x 4 = Final Price

Pricing Reflection

Were you surprised by how much your start-up costs are?

Is your menu item a good price or do you think it is too expensive for your customers?

Identify two things you learned during this module.

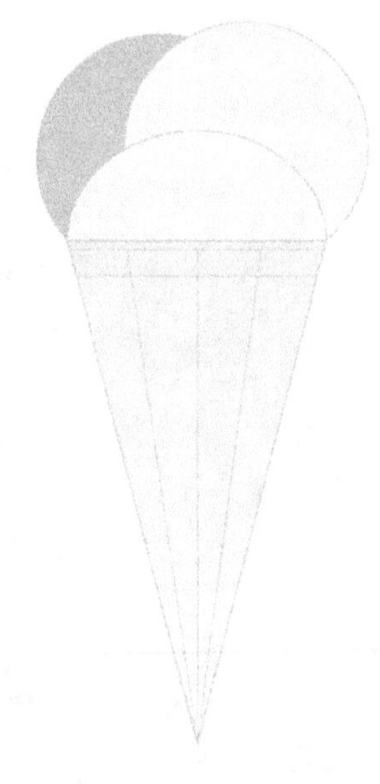

My Ice Cream Shop Instagram

Create an Instagram post to let your followers know about today's special.

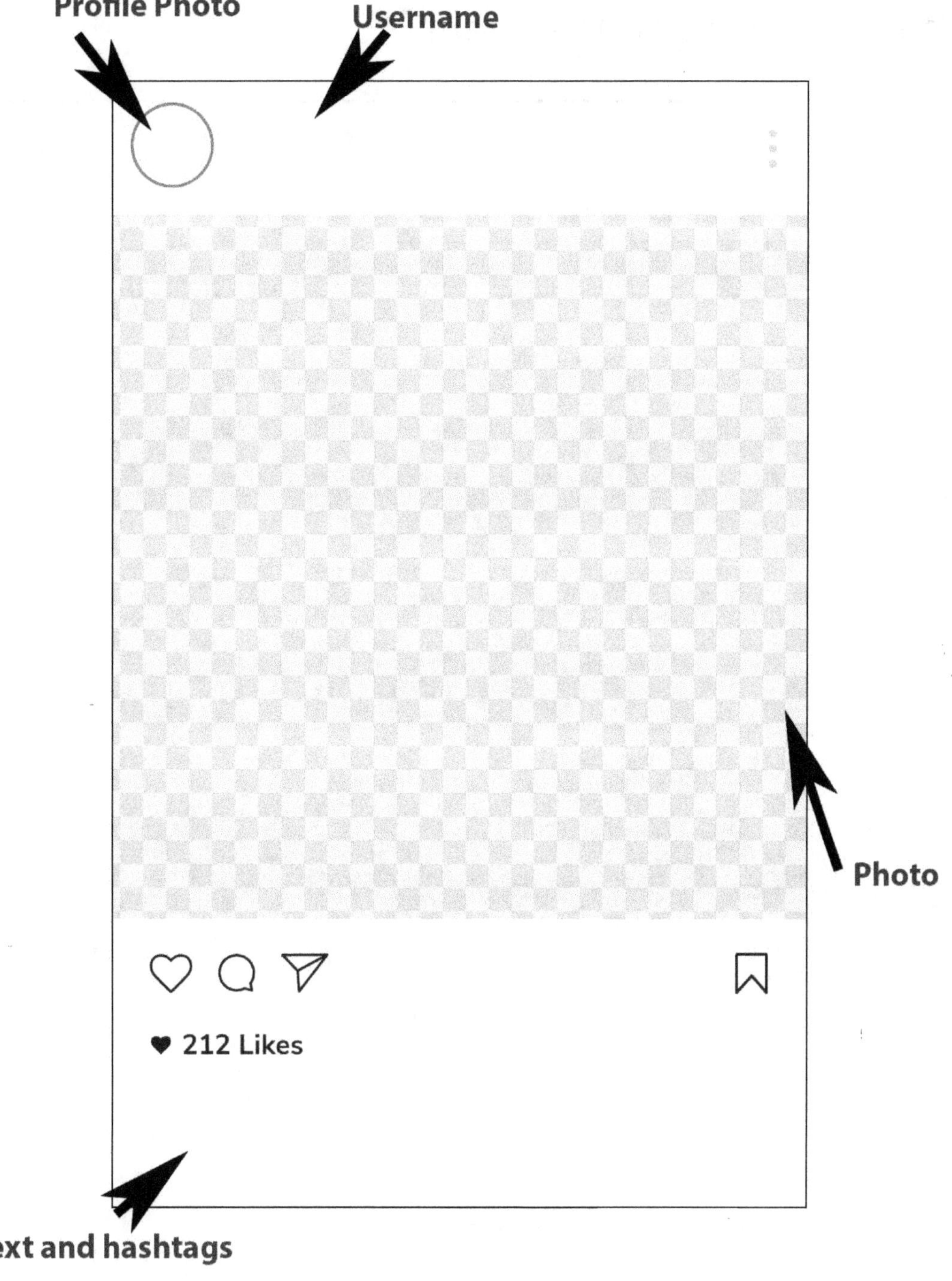

Ice Cream Shop Flyer

Your ice cream shop will be participating in the neighborhood street fair this weekend. Make up a flyer to advertise your shop and the event.

My Ice Cream Shop Website Notes

List 10 things that your customers might want to know about your ice cream shop.

1

2

3

4

5

6

7

8

9

10

My Website Design

Plan the layout of your website by listing what information will appear on each page.   Design your actual pages on separate pieces of paper.

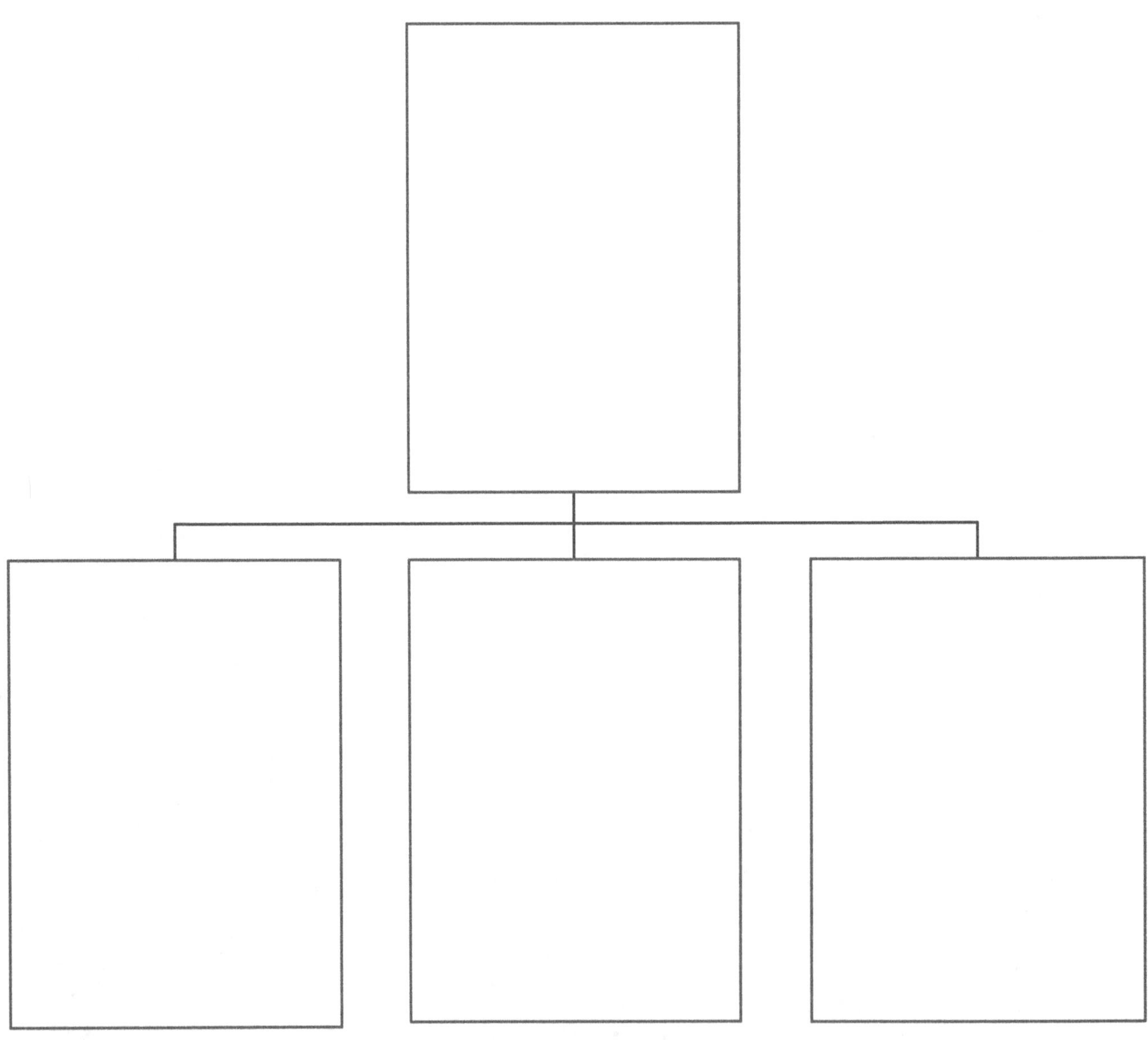

Marketing Reflection

What was the most challenging part of designing your marketing documents?

Do your marketing documents reflect your brand?

What gave you the most satisfaction in this module?

Ice Cream Shop Fair: Spending Form

Welcome to our ice cream shop fair. You have $________ to spend. Please make a purchase at a variety of shops. For each shop, please make a positive comment.

Ice cream shop Name	Amount Spent	Comment

Ice Cream Shop Order Form

Use this form to keep track of the orders at your shop.

Items Ordered	Total Cost

Ice Cream Shop Review

Why did you choose this shop to review?

Do you think the shop owner made good menu choices?

What comments can you make about the overall customer experience?

If you bought something, please comment on that experience.

How does this shop market itself?

What can you learn from this shop?

Welcome & Thank You

Thank you for coming to our presentation.

Ice cream shop:

I liked:	I wish:

Ice cream shop:

I liked:	I wish:

Ice cream shop:

I liked:	I wish:

13. You Might Also Like…

Please check out the following PBL projects from PBL Central.

Terms of Use

The usual legal stuff.... Let's put it here and then get on with the fun!!

All rights reserved. Purchase of this resource entitles the purchaser the right to reproduce the pages for use in their own classroom. Duplication for an entire school, and entire school system or for commercial purposes is strictly forbidden without written permission from the publisher. Additional licenses must be purchased for usage that extends beyond a single classroom.

Copying any part of this product and placing it on the internet in any form is strictly forbidden and is a violation of the Digital Millennium Copyright Act (DMCA).

You May:	You May Not:
Make copies for your students' use in a single classroom. Use the resources again in another of your classes once the first class is finished. Have FUN working with your students while using this resource. Feel like a great teacher for providing an awesome learning experience!	Pass this resource on to a friend/colleague. Use in multiple classes at the same time. Sell or donate the resource. Post the resource on a website of any kind. Change, copy or edit for the purpose of reselling it in any form.

 Ice Cream Shop Tycoon